BEFORE YOU BEGIN...

Make sure to download the FREE audio program for this book which comes with your purchase! Just go to

www.slangman.com/audio

then look for your book and enter this code:

E2S3PNJKAI54

Beauty and the Beast

Written by: David Burke
Copy Editor: Julie Bobrick
Illustrated by: "Migs!" Sandoval
Translator: Marcela Redoles

Copyright © 2017 by David Burke

Email: info@heywordy.com
Website: www.heywordy.com

Hey Wordy! and all related characters and elements are © and trademarks of Hey Wordy, LLC.

Published by Slangman Publishing. Slangman is a registered trademark of David Burke. All rights reserved. Reproduction or translation of any part of this work beyond that permitted by section 107 or 108 of the 1976 United States Copyright Act without the permission of the copyright owner is unlawful. Requests for permission or further information should be addressed to the Permissions Department, Slangman Publishing. This publication is designed to provide accurate and authoritative information in regard to the subject matter covered. The persons, entities and events in this book are fictitious. Any similarities with actual persons or entities, past and present, are purely coincidental.

ISBN13: 978-1-891888-39-7

Printed in the U.S.A.

Meet the Author
David Burke

Creator and star of the children's TV show, *Hey Wordy!*, David Burke has been single-handedly revolutionizing the foreign language-learning movement worldwide.

In addition to being a performer of boundless energy and enthusiasm, David speaks seven languages. A successful author and entrepreneur, he has built a thriving international publishing company featuring over 100 books he has written for teen/adults & children. His books have won publishing awards and have sold more than one million copies. David's Street Speak™ and Biz Speak™ series of books and audio programs are used around the world by government agencies, leading universities and major corporations.

Since age 4, David has been a classically trained pianist and uses his musical gifts to compose and perform original songs for his TV series, *Hey Wordy!* which introduces children to foreign languages and cultures through music, animation, and magical adventures. He has also composed, orchestrated, and performed all the music in the audio programs for each of these books.

David's engaging and charismatic persona became a fixture on broadcast entertainment channels around the world, such as CNN and the BBC. David and his work have been highlighted in many major publications, including The Los Angeles Times, The Chicago Tribune and The Christian Science Monitor.

"This series teaches everyday words that occur in your child's life, as well as terms having to do with politeness, greetings, family & friendship."

David Burke

Spanish vocabulary taught:

almuerzo = *lunch*
amable = *kind*
anillo = *ring*
bestia = *beast*
caballo = *horse*
cinco = *five*
collar = *necklace*
cuatro = *four*
feo = *ugly*
hija = *daughter*

hola = *hi*
jardín = *garden*
mediodía = *noon*
mucho = *very much*
por favor = *please*
regalo = *gift*
rosa = *rose*
seis = *six*
señor = *sir*
te quiero = *I love you*

One thing to remember...

The words in *green italics* throughout this fairy tale are words you've already learned in the previous level! Do you still remember what they mean?

from Cindellera (Level 1)

adiós = goodbye
bonita = pretty
casa = house
de nada = you're welcome
enamorado = in love
esposa = wife
feliz = happy
fiesta = party
gracias = thank you
grande = big
guapo = handsome
mala = mean
medianoche = midnight
momento = moment
muchacha = girl
pie = foot
príncipe = prince
triste = sad
vestido = dress
zapato = shoe

from Goldilocks & The Three Bears (Level 2)

bebé = baby
blanda = soft
caliente = hot
cama = bed
cansada = tired
cocina = kitchen
tazón = bowl
dos = two
dura = hard
frío = cold
mamá = mama
mesa = table
oso = bear
papá = papa
paseo = stroll
pequeño = little
puerta = door
silla = chair
tres = three
uno = one

1

Once upon a time, there was a *papá* who had an eldest (daughter) named Julie, a middle **hija** named Tessa, and a youngest **hija** named Belle. He loved them (very much). While preparing

to take a long [trip], he asked each **hija**, "What can I bring you from my **viaje**?" "I'd like a [ring] to wear on my finger," said Julie. "I'd like a [necklace] to wear around my neck." said Tessa.

viaje
anillo
collar

Por favor

rosa

But Belle, who was the most *bonita* of all said, "Please. I don't want an **anillo** to wear on my finger or a **collar** to wear around my neck. All I want is a rose." He replied, "You shall each

receive your gift." "Oh, *Gracias! Gracias!* said each **hija**. Then their *papá* mounted his horse as they shouted "Have a good **viaje**, *papá*! We will miss you **mucho**!"

→ **regalo**

→ **caballo**

As he rode off, each **hija** shouted again, "*Adiós, papá! Adiós!*" until he was out of sight. Days later, it was time for him to return. So he first stopped to buy an **anillo** for his eldest

hija to wear on her finger, a **collar** for his second **hija** to wear around her neck, but he waited to get closer to his *casa* to look for a garden where he could find a **rosa** for

jardín

Belle. After a few hours, he saw a magnificent **jardín**. He got off his **caballo**, walked into the **jardín** and picked a **rosa** that was the most **bonita** he'd ever seen. At that very **momento**,

the **puerta** to the **casa** opened and a beast → **bestia**
came out and ran toward him. "Who stole
a **rosa** from my **jardín**?" exploded the
bestia. "Oh, **por favor**, sir !" said the → **señor**

papá. "**Por favor, señor**. Don't hurt me. I promised my **hija** that I'd bring her a **rosa** as a **regalo** after my long **viaje**. It was just ONE **rosa** from your **jardín**!" "It's still

stealing!" said the **bestia**. "I will spare your life if you bring me the **hija** you speak of by noon in six days. Here she will live the rest of her life." Naturally, the

mediodía

seis

papá was very upset by this request, but he promised to return with Belle at **mediodía** in **seis** days. As he arrived home, each **hija** rushed out to greet him. He gave them each

the **regalo** they'd asked for. Each **hija** was very *feliz* and shouted, "Oh, *gracias*, *papá*! *Gracias!*" "*De nada!*" he replied. But he was still upset because he had to tell Belle

13

te quiero

about the promise he'd made with the **bestia**. "Belle, I love you. **Te quiero mucho** and want you to be *feliz*. But I must tell you what I have done…" Her *papá* went on to

explain what had happened that day and about the promise he had made. He warned her about how ugly the **bestia** was. But Belle felt responsible because the **rosa** was a **regalo**

fea

she'd requested. So, she agreed to go. The days passed quickly until it was time to leave. As Belle and her **papá** mounted the **caballo** and rode off, she was very **triste** to say **adiós** to her sisters.

After a **viaje** that took several hours, Belle and her *papá* arrived at exactly **mediodía** as instructed. They got off the **caballo** and approached the *casa* of the **bestia**.

Hola

The *puerta* opened slowly and they walked in. "Hello!" said the *papá*. "¡*Hola*!" But there was no answer. Then they saw a *mesa* filled with food in the middle of the *cocina*.

It looked like someone was having a *fiesta*! Just then they heard a deep voice say, "**Hola**. This lunch is especially for you. **Por favor**, enjoy!" Not wanting to be impolite, they began

almuerzo

eating the magnificent **almuerzo** before them. And so many desserts! Belle was so excited and already busily counting them. "…four, five, **seis**. And such wonderful desserts they were!

cuatro
cinco

She counted them again just to make sure, "*Uno*, *dos*, *tres*, **cuatro**, **cinco**, **seis**! It was true! **Seis** delicious desserts all for them! They had never seen such a wonderful

almuerzo in their lives! Suddenly, they heard footsteps approaching. There he was – the **bestia** himself. Indeed, the **bestia** was truly **fea**. Scared, Belle said, "**Hola**,

señor and *gracias* for the delicious **almuerzo**." "*De nada*," replied the **bestia**. → **amable**
He seemed very kind toward Belle. Her *papá* was permitted to come visit her

every week which made her very *feliz*. He gave Belle a kiss, mounted his **caballo**, and said, "**Adiós**, Belle. **Te quiero. Te quiero mucho**!" and rode off back to his *casa*.

At that very **momento**, the **bestia** turned toward Belle and said, "**Por favor**. What's mine is yours. I will return every day at **mediodía** to see you." He then quickly ran off, leaving Belle alone.

Because he was so **amable** toward her, Belle was no longer afraid, and was even *feliz* when he came to visit at **mediodía**. Every day, they laughed more and more and enjoyed

sharing stories with each other in the **jardín**. But one day, the **bestia** didn't arrive at **mediodía** as usual, so Belle went to look for him. She walked outside into the **jardín** and there he was

lying on the ground lifeless. Belle cried, "Oh, why did you have to die, my **bestia**? **Te quiero**! **Te quiero mucho**!" She gave him a kiss on the cheek and suddenly right before her

eyes, he awoke and was transformed into a *príncipe* who was very *guapo*, indeed! He explained to her that an evil magician had changed him into a *bestia* and only the kiss of

a *muchacha* who was truly in love with him could change him back to the *príncipe* he used to be. The next day at **mediodía**, Belle became his *esposa*, and they all lived happily ever after.

Now you're ready for Levels 4 & 5!

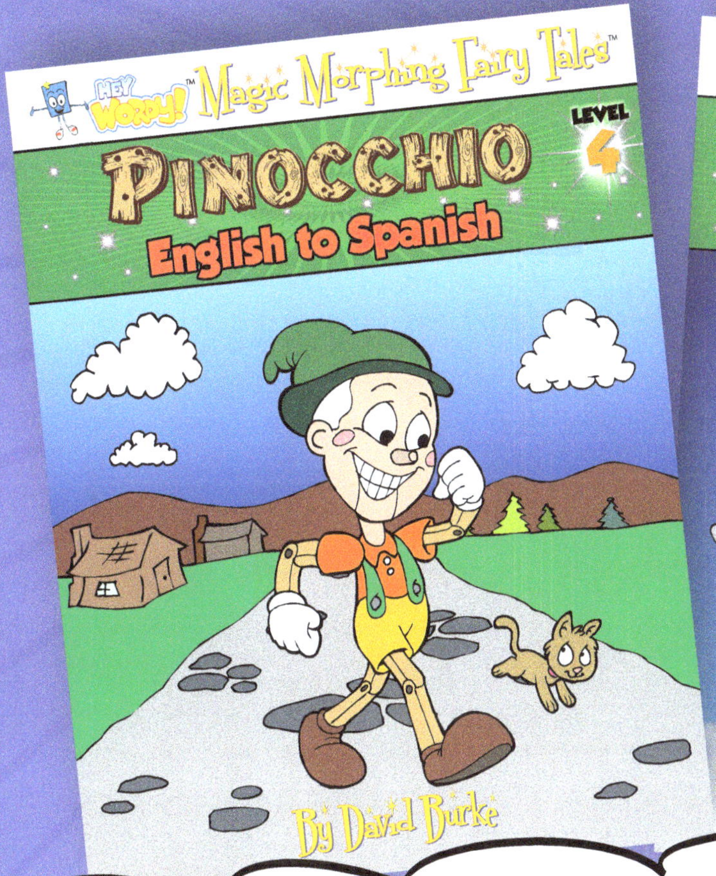

Levels 4 & 5 contain the words from Levels 1, 2 and 3 plus all NEW words!

For more HEY WORDY! products, visit...

www.HEYWORDY!.com

www.ingramcontent.com/pod-product-compliance
Lightning Source LLC
Chambersburg PA
CBHW042031100526
44587CB00029B/4368